Big Block Quilts

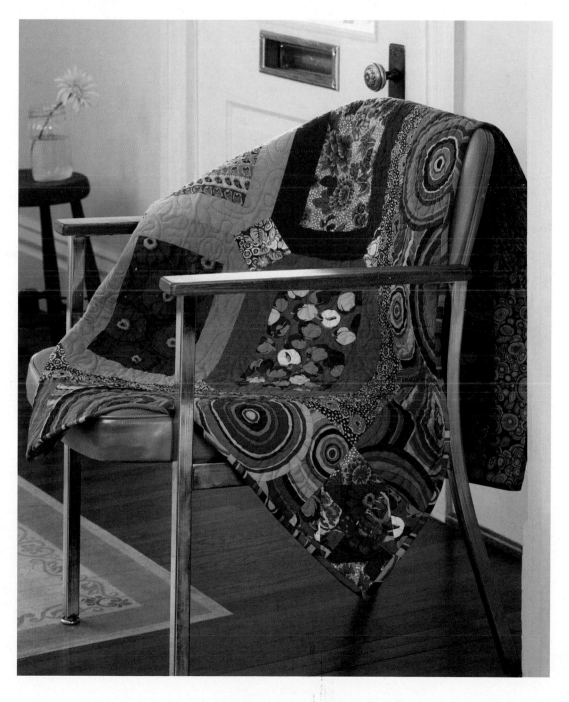

LEISURE ARTS, INC.
Maumelle, Arkansas

EDITORIAL STAFF

Senior Product Director: Pam Stebbins
Creative Art Director: Katherine Laughlin
Publications Director: Leah Lampirez
Technical Editors: Mary Sullivan Hutcheson,
    Lisa Lancaster, and Jean Lewis
Editorial Writer: Susan Frantz Wiles
Art Category Manager: Lora Puls
Prepress Technician: Stephanie Johnson

BUSINESS STAFF

President and Chief Executive Officer: Fred F. Pruss
Senior Vice President of Operations: Jim Dittrich
Vice President of Retail Sales: Martha Adams
Chief Financial Officer: Tiffany P. Childers
Controller: Teresa Eby
Information Technology Director: Brian Roden
Director of E-Commerce: Mark Hawkins
Manager of E-Commerce: Robert Young

ISBN-13/EAN: 978-1-4647-3534-9
UPC: 0-28906-06478-0

> Great for today's busy quilters, these speedy designs use large blocks or strips that go together in a weekend or less.

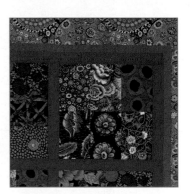

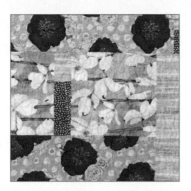

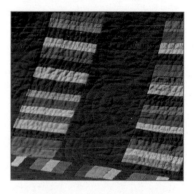

Bohemian Babe

Design by Ann D. Hansen.

Finished Quilt Size: 69" x 69" (175 cm x 175 cm)
Finished Block Size: 12" x 12" (30 cm x 30 cm)

SHOPPING LIST

Yardage is based on 43"/44" (109 cm/112 cm) wide fabric with a usable width of 40" (102 cm).

- ☐ ¹/₂ yd (46 cm) *each* of 12 assorted print fabrics
- ☐ ¹/₂ yd (46 cm) *each* of 12 assorted tone-on-tone and/or solid color fabrics
- ☐ ⁵/₈ yd (57 cm) of fabric for binding
- ☐ 4³/₈ yds (4 m) of fabric for backing
- ☐ 77" x 77" (196 cm x 196 cm) piece of batting

CUTTING

*Follow **Rotary Cutting**, page 51, to cut fabric. Cut all strips from the selvage-to-selvage width of the fabric. All measurements include ¹/₄" seam allowances.*

From *each* print fabric:
- Cut 1 square 12⁵/₈" x 12⁵/₈". Cut square in half *twice* diagonally to make 4 **triangles**.*
- Cut 2 **squares** 8¹/₂" x 8¹/₂".

From *each* assorted tone-on-tone or solid color fabric:
- Cut 5 strips 2¹/₂" wide. From these strips, cut 2 **short rectangles** 2¹/₂" x 8¹/₂", 6 **medium rectangles** 2¹/₂" x 10¹/₂", and 4 **long rectangles** 2¹/₂" x 12¹/₂".**

From fabric for binding:
- Cut 8 **binding strips** 2¹/₄" wide.

* You will need a total of 16 triangles for Side Blocks. The model was made using 2 triangles from each of 5 different fabrics and 1 triangle from each of 6 different fabrics.

** You will use a total of 64 medium rectangles and 40 long rectangles and will have 8 extra of each size.

MAKING THE BLOCKS AND SIDE BLOCKS

*Follow **Piecing**, page 52, and **Pressing**, page 53. Match the right sides and use a ¹/₄" seam allowance when sewing.*

1. For each Block you will need, 1 **short rectangle**, 2 **medium rectangles**, and 1 **long rectangle** from one fabric and 1 **square** from a contrasting fabric.

2. Sew **short rectangle** to the right edge of **square** to make **Unit 1**.

Unit 1

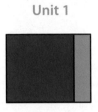

3. Turn Unit 1 one quarter turn to the left. Sew 1 **medium rectangle** to the right edge to make **Unit 2**.

Unit 2

4. Turn Unit 2 one quarter turn to the left. Sew 1 **medium rectangle** to the right edge to make **Unit 3**.

Unit 3

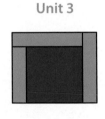

5. Turn Unit 3 one quarter turn to the left. Sew **long rectangle** to the right edge to make **Block**. Make 24 Blocks.

Block (make 24)

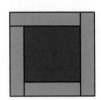

6. For each Side Block you will need, 1 **medium rectangle** and 1 **long rectangle** from one fabric and 1 **triangle** from a contrasting fabric.

7. Sew **medium rectangle** to 1 short edge of **triangle** to make **Unit 4**.

Unit 4

8. Sew **long rectangle** to remaining short edge of triangle *(Fig. 1)*. Trim rectangles even with long edge of triangle to make **Side Block**. Make 16 Side Blocks.

Fig. 1   **Side Block** (make 16)

          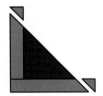

ASSEMBLING THE QUILT TOP

*Refer to **Assembly Diagram** to assemble the quilt top.*

1. Arrange Blocks and Side Blocks into 8 diagonal rows. Label rows 1-8.

2. Keeping block placement the same as your arrangement, sew Blocks and Side Blocks together into **Rows**.

3. Sew Rows together to make Quilt Top.

COMPLETING THE QUILT

1. Follow **Quilting**, page 55, to mark, layer, and quilt as desired. The model is machine quilted with an all-over flower and leaf pattern.

2. If desired, follow **Adding A Hanging Sleeve**, page 59, to add a hanging sleeve.

3. Use **binding strips** and follow **Piecing Binding Strips**, page 60, and **Attaching Binding with Mitered Corners**, page 61, to make and attach **straight-grain binding**.

Assembly Diagram

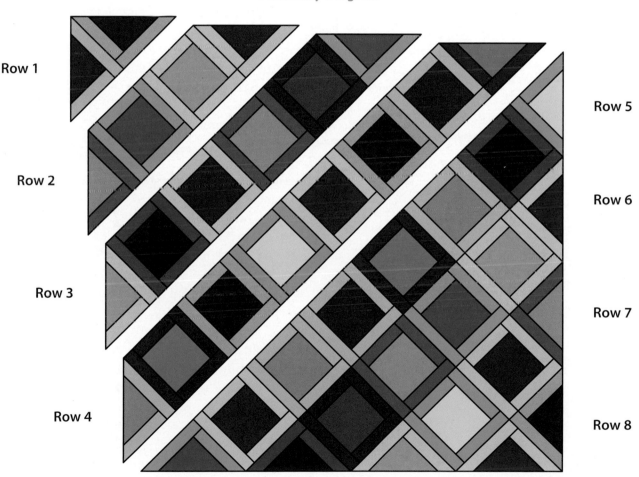

Row 1

Row 2

Row 3

Row 4

Row 5

Row 6

Row 7

Row 8

Simple Elegance

Design by Ann D. Hansen.

Finished Quilt Size: 57" x 70¹/₂" (145 cm x 179 cm)
Finished Block Size: 12" x 12" (30 cm x 30 cm)

SHOPPING LIST

Yardage is based on 43"/44" (109 cm/112 cm) wide fabric with a usable width of 40" (102 cm). Fat quarters are approximately 21" x 18" (53 cm x 46 cm).

- ☐ 12 assorted fat quarters
- ☐ ³/₄ yd (69 cm) of orange solid fabric
- ☐ ³/₈ yd (34 cm) of gold solid fabric
- ☐ 2¹/₄ yds (2.1 m) of gold print fabric
- ☐ 4³/₈ yds (4 m) of fabric for backing
- ☐ 65" x 78" (165 cm x 198 cm) piece of batting

CUTTING

*Follow **Rotary Cutting**, page 51, to cut fabric. Cut all strips from the selvage-to-selvage width of the fabric. All measurements include ¹/₄" seam allowances.*

From *each* fat quarter:
- Cut 6 **rectangles** 4¹/₂" x 6¹/₂". Stack rectangles from each fat quarter together.

From orange solid fabric:
- Cut 6 strips 2" wide. From these strips, cut 16 **short sashing strips** 2" x 12¹/₂".
- Cut 5 **long sashing strips** 2" x 42¹/₂", piecing as necessary.

From gold solid fabric:
- Cut 2 **side inner borders** 1¹/₂" x 56", piecing as necessary.
- Cut 2 **top/bottom inner borders** 1¹/₂" x 44¹/₂", piecing as necessary.

From gold print fabric:
- Cut 7 **binding strips** 2¹/₄" wide.
- Cut 2 *lengthwise* **top/bottom outer borders** 6¹/₂" x 56¹/₂".
- Cut 2 *lengthwise* **side outer borders** 6¹/₂" x 58".

MAKING THE BLOCKS

*Follow **Piecing**, page 52, and **Pressing**, page 53. Match the right sides and use a ¹/₄" seam allowance when sewing.*

1. Divide stacks of **rectangles** into 2 groups of 6 stacks each.

2. Using 1 rectangle from each stack in group 1, refer to **Block A Diagram** to make **Block A**. Keeping fabric placement the same in each block, make 6 Block A's.

Block A (make 6)

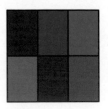

3. Referring to **Block B Diagram**, repeat Step 2 using 1 rectangle from each stack in group 2 to make **Block B**. Make 6 Block B's.

Block B (make 6)

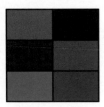

ASSEMBLING THE QUILT TOP

*Refer to **Quilt Top Diagram** to assemble the quilt top.*

1. Sew 2 Block A's, 1 Block B, and 4 **short sashing strips** together to make **Row 1**. Make 2 Row 1's.

Row 1 (make 2)

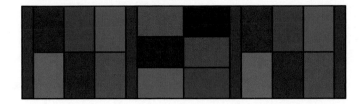

2. Sew 2 Block B's, 1 Block A, and 4 short sashing strips together to make **Row 2**. Make 2 Row 2's.

Row 2 (make 2)

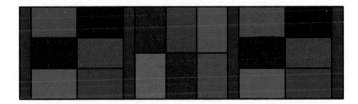

3. Sew Rows and 5 **long sashing strips** together to make **Quilt Top Center**.

4. Matching centers and corners, sew **side** then **top/bottom inner borders** to Quilt Top Center.

5. Matching centers and corners, sew **side** then **top/bottom outer borders** to Quilt Top Center to complete **Quilt Top**.

COMPLETING THE QUILT

1. Follow **Quilting**, page 55, to mark, layer, and quilt as desired. The model is machine quilted with an all-over swirl pattern.

2. If desired, follow **Adding A Hanging Sleeve**, page 59, to add a hanging sleeve.

3. Use **binding strips** and follow **Piecing Binding Strips**, page 60, and **Attaching Binding with Mitered Corners**, page 61, to make and attach **straight-grain binding**.

Quilt Top Diagram

Point Taken

Design by Ann D. Hansen.

Finished Quilt Size: 44" x 62" (112 cm x 157 cm)
Finished Block Size: 9" x 9" (23 cm x 23 cm)

SHOPPING LIST

Yardage is based on 43"/44" (109 cm/112 cm) wide fabric with a usable width of 40" (102 cm). Fat quarters are approximately 21" x 18" (53 cm x 46 cm).

- ☐ 12 assorted stripe fat quarters*
- ☐ 12 solid color fat quarters*
- ☐ 1/2 yd (46 cm) of fabric for binding
- ☐ 4 yds (3.7 m) of fabric for backing
- ☐ 52" x 70" (132 cm x 178 cm) piece of batting

* Model was made using 1 fat quarter *each* of 6 assorted fabrics and 2 fat quarters *each* of 3 assorted fabrics.

CUTTING

*Follow **Rotary Cutting**, page 51, to cut fabric. Cut all strips from fat quarters across the 21" width of fabric. Cut binding strips from the selvage-to-selvage width of the fabric. All measurements include 1/4" seam allowances.*

From *each* assorted stripe fat quarter:
- Cut 2 strips 3 1/2" wide. From these strips, cut 2 **rectangles** 3 1/2" x 9 1/2", 3 **squares** 3 1/2" x 3 1/2", and 2 **small squares** 1 1/2" x 1 1/2".

From remainder of stripe fat quarters:
- Cut a *total* of 10 **border rectangles** 4" x 18 1/2".
- Cut a *total* of 4 **assorted corner squares** 4" x 4".

From *each* solid color fat quarter:
- Cut 2 strips 3 1/2" wide. From these strips, cut 2 **rectangles** 3 1/2" x 9 1/2", 3 **squares** 3 1/2" x 3 1/2", and 2 **small squares** 1 1/2" x 1 1/2".

From remainder of solid color fat quarters:
- Cut a *total* of 10 sets of 2 **matching border squares** and a *total* of 4 **assorted border squares** 1 1/2" x 1 1/2".

From binding fabric:
- Cut 6 **binding strips** 2 1/4" wide.

MAKING THE BLOCKS

*Follow **Piecing**, page 52, and **Pressing**, page 53. Match the right sides and use a ¼" seam allowance when sewing. **Note:** Each pair of adjacent blocks has the exact opposite placement of the same 2 fabrics.*

1. For each pair of blocks, select 2 **rectangles**, 3 **squares**, and 2 **small squares** from one stripe fabric. Select the same pieces from one solid fabric.

2. Sew 1 stripe and 2 solid **squares** together to make **Unit 1**.

Unit 1

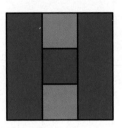

3. Sew 1 stripe **rectangle** to either side of Unit 1 to make **Unit 2**.

Unit 2

4. Refer to **Fig. 1** to position and sew 1 solid **small square** to 2 corners of Unit 2. Trim seam allowances to ¼"; press open to complete **Block A**.

Fig. 1

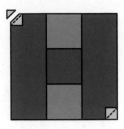

Block A

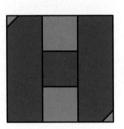

5. Using remaining rectangles, squares, and small squares selected in Step 1 and reversing fabric placement as shown, repeat Steps 2-4 to make **Block B**.

Block B

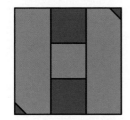

6. Repeat Steps 1-5 to make a total of 12 *pairs* of Blocks.

ASSEMBLING THE QUILT TOP

*Refer to **Quilt Top Diagram**, page 17, to assemble the quilt top.*

1. Sew each pair of Blocks together. Sew 2 pairs of Blocks together to make **Row**. Make 6 Rows.

Row

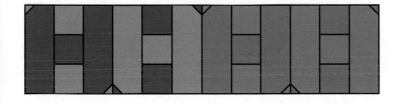

2. Sew Rows together to complete **Quilt Top Center**.

3. Refer to Step 4 of **Making The Blocks** to sew one set of matching **border squares** to one **border rectangle** to make **Unit 3**. Make 10 Unit 3's.

Unit 3 (make 10)

4. In the same manner, sew one **border square** to one **corner square** to make **Unit 4**. Make 4 Unit 4's.

Unit 4 (make 4)

5. Sew 3 Unit 3's together to make **Side Border**. Make 2 Side Borders.

Side Border (make 2)

6. Sew 2 Unit 3's and 2 Unit 4's together to make **Top/Bottom Border**. Make 2 Top/Bottom Borders.

Top/Bottom Border (make 2)

7. Matching centers and corners, sew **side**, and then **top/bottom borders** to Quilt Top Center to complete **Quilt Top**.

COMPLETING THE QUILT

1. Follow **Quilting**, page 55, to mark, layer, and quilt as desired. The model is machine quilted with an all-over leaf pattern.

2. If desired, follow **Adding A Hanging Sleeve**, page 59, to add a hanging sleeve.

3. Use **binding strips** and follow **Piecing Binding Strips**, page 60, and **Attaching Binding with Mitered Corners**, page 61, to make and attach **straight-grain binding**.

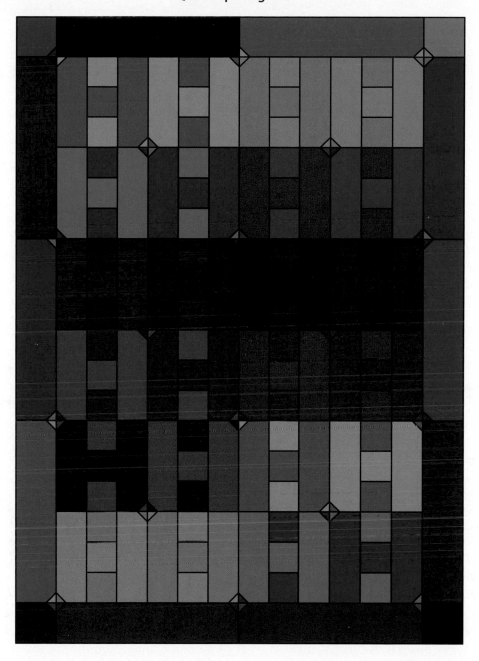

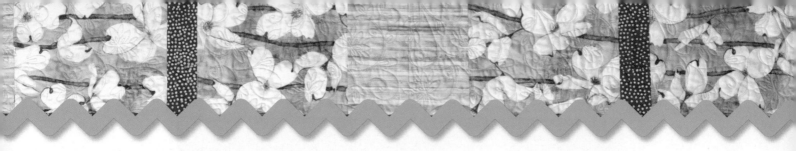

Mod About You

Design by Ann D. Hansen.

Finished Quilt Size: 61" x 82" (155 cm x 208 cm)
Finished Block Size: 30" x 40¹/₂" (76 cm x 103 cm)

SHOPPING LIST

Yardage is based on 43"/44" (109 cm/112 cm) wide fabric with a usable width of 40" (102 cm).

- ☐ 2¹/₈ yds (1.9 m) of blue floral print fabric
- ☐ 2 yds (1.8 m) of green floral print fabric
- ☐ 1¹/₄ yds (1.1 m) of green stripe fabric
- ☐ ⁷/₈ yd (80 cm) of red dot fabric
- ☐ 5 yds (4.6 m) of fabric for backing
- ☐ 69" x 90" (175 cm x 229 cm) piece of batting

CUTTING

*Follow **Rotary Cutting**, page 51, to cut fabric. Cut all strips from the selvage-to-selvage width of the fabric. All measurements include ¹/₄" seam allowances.*

From blue floral print fabric:
- Cut 2 strips 22¹/₂" wide. From these strips, cut 4 **A rectangles** 22¹/₂" x 15¹/₂".
- Cut 4 strips 6" wide. From these strips, cut 4 **C rectangles** 6" x 26¹/₂".

From green floral print fabric:
- Cut 6 strips 10¹/₂" wide. From these strips, cut 16 **B squares** 10¹/₂" x 10¹/₂".

From green stripe fabric:
- Cut 8 strips 4¹/₂" wide. From these strips, cut 8 **D rectangles** 4¹/₂" x 35¹/₂".*
- Cut 2 strips 2¹/₂" wide. From these strips, cut 4 **E rectangles** 2¹/₂" x 2", 4 **F rectangles** 2¹/₂" x 4", 4 **G rectangles** 2¹/₂" x 3¹/₄", and 4 **H rectangles** 2¹/₂" x 4¹/₂".

From red dot fabric:
- Cut 3 strips 2¹/₂" wide. From these strips, cut 4 **I rectangles** 2¹/₂" x 9", 4 **J rectangles** 2¹/₂" x 7", 4 **K rectangles** 2¹/₂" x 3¹/₄", and 4 **L rectangles** 2¹/₂" x 2".
- Cut 8 **binding strips** 2¹/₄" wide.

* To perfectly match the stripes of D rectangles from block to block, first cut all strips across the width of the fabric. From 1 strip, cut the size rectangle needed. Working with 1 strip at a time, align the stripes of each remaining strip with the first rectangle; trim the strip to match the first rectangle.

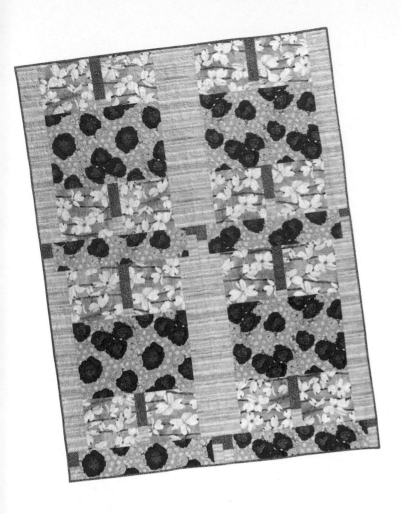

3. Matching short edges, sew 1 **F rectangle** and 1 **J rectangle** together to make **Unit 3**. Make 4 Unit 3's.

Unit 3 (make 4)

4. Sew 1 **B square** to either side of 1 Unit 3 to make **Unit 4**. Make 4 Unit 4's.

Unit 4 (make 4)

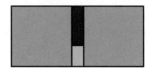

5. Sew 1 Unit 2, 1 **A rectangle** and 1 Unit 4 together to make **Unit 5**. Make 4 Unit 5's.

Unit 5 (make 4)

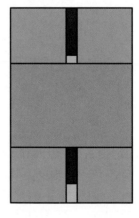

MAKING THE BLOCKS

*Follow **Piecing**, page 52, and **Pressing**, page 53. Match the right sides and use a ¹/₄" seam allowance when sewing.*

1. Sew 1 **E rectangle** and 1 **I rectangle** together to make **Unit 1**. Make 4 Unit 1's.

Unit 1 (make 4)

2. Sew 1 **B square** to either side of 1 Unit 1 to make **Unit 2**. Make 4 Unit 2's.

Unit 2 (make 4)

6. Sew 1 **D rectangle** to either side of 1 Unit 5 to make **Unit 6**. Make 4 Unit 6's.

Unit 6 (make 4)

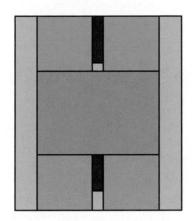

7. Matching short edges, sew 1 **G rectangle** and 1 **K rectangle** together to make **Unit 7**. Make 4 Unit 7's.

Unit 7 (make 4)

8. Sew 1 **H rectangle** and 1 **L rectangle** together to make **Unit 8**. Make 4 Unit 8's.

Unit 8 (make 4)

9. Sew 1 Unit 7 to the left side and 1 Unit 8 to the right side of 1 **C rectangle** to make **Unit 9**. Make 4 Unit 9's.

Unit 9 (make 4)

10. Sew 1 Unit 9 to the bottom edge of 1 Unit 6 to complete **Block**. Make 4 Blocks.

Block (make 4)

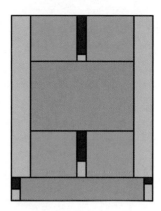

ASSEMBLING THE QUILT TOP
*Refer to **Quilt Top Diagram**, page 22, to assemble the quilt top.*

1. Sew 2 Blocks together to make **Row**. Make 2 Rows.

Row (make 2)

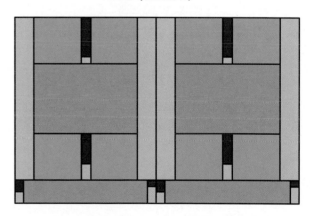

2. Sew Rows together to complete **Quilt Top**.

COMPLETING THE QUILT

1. Follow **Quilting**, page 55, to mark, layer, and quilt as desired. The model is machine quilted with an all-over flower and vine pattern.

2. If desired, follow **Adding A Hanging Sleeve**, page 59, to add a hanging sleeve.

3. Use **binding strips** and follow **Piecing Binding Strips**, page 60, and **Attaching Binding with Mitered Corners**, page 61, to make and attach **straight-grain binding**.

Quilt Top Diagram

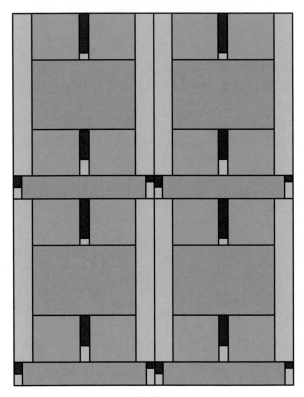

Small Mod
Design by Ann D. Hansen.

Finished Quilt Size: 31" x 41½" (79 cm x 105 cm)

SHOPPING LIST

Yardage is based on 43"/44" (109 cm/112 cm) wide fabric with a usable width of 40" (102 cm).

- ☐ 22½" x 15½" (57 cm x 39 cm) **A rectangle** of black floral print fabric
- ☐ 26½" x 6" (67 cm x 15 cm) **C rectangle** of black/white dot fabric
- ☐ ³/₈ yd (34 cm) of black print fabric
- ☐ ³/₈ yd (34 cm) of green dot fabric
- ☐ ³/₄ yd (69 cm) of pink print fabric
- ☐ ¹/₈ yd (11 cm) of pink/white print fabric
- ☐ 1³/₈ yds (1.3 m) of fabric for backing
- ☐ 39" x 49" (99 cm x 124 cm) piece of batting

CUTTING

*Follow **Rotary Cutting**, page 51, to cut fabric. Cut all strips from the selvage-to-selvage width of the fabric. All measurements include ¼" seam allowances.*

From black print fabric:
- Cut 1 strip 2½" wide. From this strip, cut 1 **F rectangle** 2½" x 4", 1 **G rectangle** 2½" x 3¼", 1 **H rectangle** 2½" x 4½", and 1 **I rectangle** 2½" x 9".
- Cut 4 **binding strips** 2¼" wide.

From green dot fabric:
- Cut 2 strips 4½" wide. From these strips, cut 2 **D rectangles** 4½" x 35½".

From pink print fabric:
- Cut 2 strips 10½" wide. From these strips, cut 4 **B squares** 10½" x 10½".

From pink/white print fabric:
- Cut 1 strip 2½" wide. From this strip, cut 1 **E rectangle** 2½" x 2", 1 **J rectangle** 2½" x 7", 1 **K rectangle** 2½" x 3¼", and 1 **L rectangle** 2½" x 2".

MAKING THE BLOCKS

*Referring to the photos, left and right, for fabric placement, follow **Making the Blocks**, page 20, to make the quilt top.*

Quilt Top Diagram

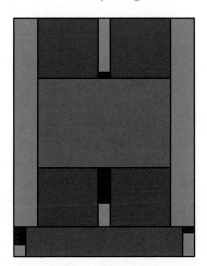

COMPLETING THE QUILT

*Follow **Completing The Quilt**, page 22, to complete the quilt. The model is machine quilted with an all-over leaf and loop pattern.*

Picture This

Design by Ann D. Hansen.

Finished Quilt Size: 47" x 59" (119 cm x 150 cm)
Finished Block Size: 10" x 14" (25 cm x 36 cm)

SHOPPING LIST

Yardage is based on 43"/44" (109 cm/112 cm) wide fabric with a usable width of 40" (102 cm). Fat quarters are approximately 21" x 18" (53 cm x 46 cm).

- ☐ 6 assorted print fat quarters
- ☐ 6 solid color fat quarters
- ☐ 7" x 7" (18 cm x 18 cm) square *each of 4* assorted small print fabrics
- ☐ $1/2$ yd (46 cm) of fabric for inner border
- ☐ $1^7/8$ yds (1.7 m) of fabric for outer border and binding
- ☐ $3^3/4$ yds (3.4 m) of fabric for backing
- ☐ 55" x 67" (140 cm x 170 cm) piece of batting

CUTTING

*Follow **Rotary Cutting**, page 51, to cut fabric. Cut all strips from the selvage-to-selvage width of the fabric. All measurements include $1/4$" seam allowances.*

From assorted print fat quarters:
- Cut a *total* of 9 **block centers** $6^1/2$" x $10^1/2$".*

  From *each* of 4 assorted print fat quarters:
  - Cut 4 **large squares** 4" x 4".

From *each* of 3 solid color fat quarters:
- Cut 4 **long rectangles** $2^1/2$" x $10^1/2$".
- Cut 4 **short rectangles** $2^1/2$" x $6^1/2$".
- Cut 4 **squares** 3" x 3".

  From *each* of 3 remaining solid color fat quarters:
  - Cut 2 **long rectangles** $2^1/2$" x $10^1/2$".
  - Cut 2 **short rectangles** $2^1/2$" x $6^1/2$".
  - Cut 2 **squares** 3" x 3".

From assorted small print squares:
- Cut 9 *sets* of 2 matching **squares** 3" x 3".

From inner border fabric:
- Cut 2 **side inner borders** $2^1/2$" x $42^1/2$", piecing as necessary.
- Cut 2 **top/bottom inner borders** $2^1/2$" x $34^1/2$".

From outer border and binding fabric:
- Cut 6 **binding strips** $2^1/4$" wide.
- Cut 2 *lengthwise* **top/bottom outer borders** $6^1/2$" x $34^1/2$".
- Cut 2 *lengthwise* **side outer borders** $6^1/2$" x $46^1/2$".

* Model was made using 2 centers from *each* of 3 print fat quarters and 1 center from *each* of the 3 remaining print fat quarters.

MAKING THE BLOCKS

*Follow **Piecing**, page 52, and **Pressing**, page 53. Match the right sides and use a ¼" seam allowance when sewing.*

1. For each block, select 1 **block center** and 1 set of small print **squares**. From one solid color fabric, select 2 **long rectangles**, 2 **short rectangles**, and 2 **squares**.

2. Draw a diagonal line on wrong side of each solid color square.

3. Matching right sides, place 1 marked square on top of 1 unmarked square. Stitch ¼" from each side of drawn line *(Fig. 1)*. Cut along drawn line and press seam allowances toward darker fabric to make 2 **Small Triangle-Squares**. Trim each Small Triangle-Square to 2½" x 2½". Make 4 Small Triangle-Squares.

Fig. 1

Small Triangle-Square (make 4)

4. Sew 1 **long rectangle** to either side of block center to make **Unit 1**.

Unit 1

5. Sew 1 Small Triangle-Square to each end of 1 short rectangle to make **Unit 2**. Make 2 Unit 2's.

Unit 2 (make 2)

6. Sew 1 Unit 2 to top and bottom edges of Unit 1 to complete **Block**.

Block (make 9)

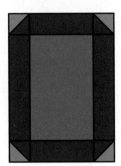

7. Repeat Steps 1-6 to make a total of 9 Blocks.

ASSEMBLING THE QUILT TOP

*Refer to **Quilt Top Diagram**, page 29, to assemble the quilt top.*

1. Sew 3 Blocks together to make **Row**. Make 3 Rows. **Note:** Rows 1 and 3 of the model are the same 3 blocks in reverse order.

Row (make 3)

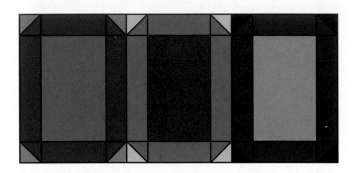

2. Sew rows together to complete **Quilt Top Center**.

3. Matching centers and corners, sew **side** then **top/bottom inner borders** to Quilt Top Center.

4. Draw a diagonal line on the wrong side of 4 **large squares** from each of 2 print fabrics.

5. Select 4 matching marked large squares and 4 matching unmarked large squares. Match the right sides and place 1 marked large square on top of 1 unmarked large square. Stitch ¹/₄" from each side of drawn line *(Fig. 2)*. Cut along drawn line and press seam allowances toward darker fabric to make 2 **Large Triangle-Square A's**. Trim each Large Triangle-Square A to 3¹/₂" x 3¹/₂". Make 8 Large Triangle-Square A's.

Fig. 2

Large Triangle-Square A (make 8)

6. Use the remaining marked and unmarked large squares to make 8 **Large Triangle-Square B's**. Trim each Large Triangle-Square B to 3¹/₂" x 3¹/₂".

Large Triangle-Square B (make 8)

7. Sew 2 Large Triangle-Square A's and 2 Large Triangle-Square B's together to make **corner square**. Make 4 corner squares.

Corner Square (make 4)

8. Matching centers and corners, sew **side outer borders** to Quilt Top Center.

9. Sew 1 corner square to each end of each **top/bottom border**. Sew top/bottom borders to Quilt Top Center to complete **Quilt Top**.

COMPLETING THE QUILT

1. Follow **Quilting**, page 55, to mark, layer, and quilt as desired. The model is machine quilted with an all-over meandering pattern.

2. If desired, follow **Adding A Hanging Sleeve**, page 59, to add a hanging sleeve.

3. Use **binding strips** and follow **Piecing Binding Strips**, page 60, and **Attaching Binding with Mitered Corners**, page 61, to make and attach **straight-grain binding**.

Quilt Top Diagram

Picture This, Too!

Design by Ann D. Hansen.

Finished Quilt Size:
47" x 59" (119 cm x 150 cm)
Finished Block Size:
10" x 14" (25 cm x 36 cm)

SHOPPING LIST

Yardage is based on 43"/44" (109 cm/112 cm) wide fabric with a usable width of 40" (102 cm). Fat quarters are approximately 21" x 18" (53 cm x 46 cm).

- ☐ 4 assorted large print fat quarters
- ☐ ⁵/₈ yd (57 cm) of solid color fabric
- ☐ ³/₄ yd (69 cm) of small print fabric
- ☐ ¹/₂ yd (46 cm) of fabric for inner border

- ☐ 1³/₈ yds (1.3 m) of fabric for outer border
- ☐ ³/₄ yd (69 cm) of stripe fabric for binding
- ☐ 3³/₄ yds (3.4 m) of fabric for backing
- ☐ 55" x 67" (140 cm x 170 cm) piece of batting

CUTTING

*Follow **Rotary Cutting**, page 51, to cut fabric. Cut all strips from the selvage-to-selvage width of the fabric. All measurements include ¹/₄" seam allowances.*

From assorted large print fat quarters:
- Cut a *total* of 9 **block centers** 6¹/₂" x 10¹/₂".*

From *each* of 4 assorted large print fat quarters:
  - Cut 1 *set* of 4 **matching large squares** 4" x 4".

From solid color fabric:
- Cut 5 strips 2¹/₂" wide. From these strips, cut 8 **long rectangles** 2¹/₂" x 10¹/₂" and 8 **short rectangles** 2¹/₂" x 6¹/₂".
- Cut 2 strips 3" wide. From these strips, cut 18 **squares** 3" x 3".

From small print fabric:
- Cut 6 strips 2¹/₂" wide. From these strips, cut 10 **long rectangles** 2¹/₂" x 10¹/₂" and 10 **short rectangles** 2¹/₂" x 6¹/₂".
- Cut 2 strips 3" wide. From these strips, cut 18 **squares** 3" x 3".

From inner border fabric:
- Cut 2 **side inner borders** 2¹/₂" x 42¹/₂", piecing as necessary.
- Cut 2 **top/bottom inner borders** 2¹/₂" x 34¹/₂".

From outer border fabric:
- Cut 2 *lengthwise* **top/bottom outer borders** 6¹/₂" x 34¹/₂".
- Cut 2 *lengthwise* **side outer borders** 6¹/₂" x 46¹/₂".

From binding fabric:
- Cut a **square** 23" x 23".

* Model was made using 2 centers from *each* of 3 fat quarters and 3 centers from the remaining fat quarter.

MAKING THE BLOCKS

*Referring to the **Quilt Top Diagram**, below, for fabric placement, follow **Making The Blocks**, page 26, to make 9 Blocks.*

Block (make 9)

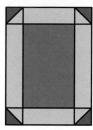

ASSEMBLING THE QUILT TOP

*Follow **Assembling The Quilt Top**, page 28, to assemble the quilt top.*

COMPLETING THE QUILT

1. Follow Steps 1-2 of **Completing The Quilt**, page 29. The model is machine quilted with an all-over meandering pattern.

2. Use **binding square** and follow **Making Continuous Bias Binding**, page 59, and **Attaching Binding with Mitered Corners**, page 61, to make and attach **binding**.

Quilt Top Diagram

Deep Blue Ocean

Design by Pat Sloan.

Finished Quilt Size: 65" x 73" (165 cm x 185 cm)
Finished Block Size: 8" x 8" (20 cm x 20 cm)

SHOPPING LIST

Yardage is based on 43"/44" (109 cm/112 cm) wide fabric with a usable width of 40" (102 cm).

- ☐ 4 yds (3.7 m) of white print #1 (blocks, inner and outer borders)*
- ☐ 3/8 yd (34 cm) of white print #2 (blocks)
- ☐ 3/8 yd (34 cm) of white print #3 (blocks)
- ☐ 1 1/2 yds (1.4 m) of blue print #1 (middle border, binding, and blocks)
- ☐ 3/8 yd (34 cm) of blue print #2 (blocks)
- ☐ 3/8 yd (34 cm) of blue print #3 (blocks)
- ☐ 4 1/2 yds (4.1 m) of fabric for backing
- ☐ 73" x 81" (185 cm x 206 cm) piece of batting

* We used a white and blue toile with a directional print that required additional fabric. If your fabric is not directional and you cut and piece the borders from the crosswise grain, you will only need 2 1/2 yds.

CUTTING THE PIECES

*Follow **Rotary Cutting**, page 51, to cut fabric. Cut all strips from the selvage-to-selvage width of the fabric unless otherwise noted. Cutting lengths for borders are exact. All measurements include 1/4" seam allowances.*

From white print #1:
- Cut 16 **strips** 1 1/2" wide.
- Cut 2 *crosswise* **top/bottom inner borders** 1 1/2" x 40 1/2", piecing as necessary.
- Cut 2 *crosswise* **top/bottom outer borders** 10" x 45 1/2", piecing as necessary.
- Cut 2 *lengthwise* **side inner borders** 1 1/2" x 50 1/2".
- Cut 2 *lengthwise* **side outer borders** 10" x 72 1/2".

From white print #2:
- Cut 8 **strips** 1 1/2" wide.

From white print #3:
- Cut 8 **strips** 1 1/2" wide.

From blue print #1:
- Cut 16 **strips** 1 1/2" wide.
- Cut 2 *crosswise* **top/bottom middle borders** 2" x 42 1/2", piecing as necessary.
- Cut 2 *crosswise* **side middle borders** 2" x 53 1/2", piecing as necessary.
- Cut 8 **binding strips** 1 1/2" wide.

From blue print #2:
- Cut 8 **strips** 1 1/2" wide.

From blue print #3:
- Cut 8 **strips** 1 1/2" wide.

MAKING THE BLOCKS

*Follow **Piecing**, page 52, and **Pressing**, page 53. Match the right sides and use a ¼" seam allowance when sewing.*

1. Alternating blue and white prints, sew 8 **strips** together to make a **Strip Set**. Make 8 Strip Sets. **Note:** 1 blue and 1 white fabric will be repeated in each Strip Set.

2. Cut across each Strip Set at 8½" intervals to make **Blocks**. Make 30 Blocks.

Strip Set (make 8)

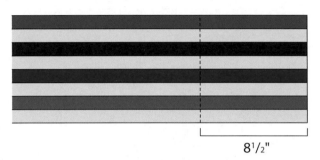

8½"

Block (make 30)

ASSEMBLING THE QUILT TOP CENTER

*Refer to **Quilt Top Diagram** for placement.*

1. Sew 5 Blocks together to make **Row 1**. Make 3 Row 1's.

2. Sew 5 Blocks together to make **Row 2**. Make 3 Row 2's.

3. Alternating Rows 1 and 2, sew Rows together to make **Quilt Top Center**.

Row 1 (make 3)

Row 2 (make 3)

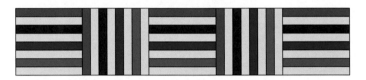

Quilt Top Diagram

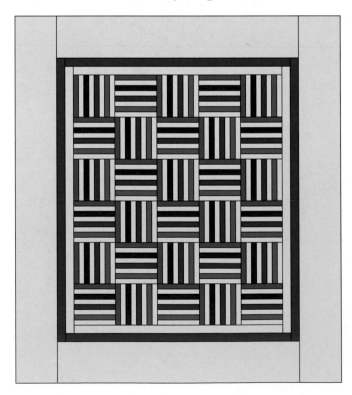

ADDING THE BORDERS

1. Matching centers and corners, sew **top/bottom inner borders** to Quilt Top Center.

2. Matching centers and corners, sew **side inner borders** to Quilt Top Center.

3. Sew **top/bottom** and **side middle** then **outer borders** to Quilt Top Center to complete the **Quilt Top**.

COMPLETING THE QUILT

1. Follow **Quilting**, page 55, to mark, layer, and quilt as desired. The model is machine quilted with horizontal and vertical swirls in the Blocks. There is outline quilting around the Blocks and in the inner and middle borders. There are wavy lines in the middle border. The outer border is quilted with a large leaf and vine pattern.

2. If desired, follow **Adding A Hanging Sleeve**, page 59, to add a hanging sleeve.

3. Use **binding strips** and follow **Piecing Binding Strips**, page 60, and **Attaching Binding with Mitered Corners**, page 61, to make and attach **straight-grain binding**.

Star Search

Design by Me & My Sister Designs, Barbara Groves & Mary Jacobson.

Finished Quilt Size: 68¹/₂" x 68¹/₂" (174 cm x 174 cm)
Finished Block Size: 6¹/₈" x 6¹/₈" (16 cm x 16 cm)

CUTTING OUT THE PIECES

*Follow **Rotary Cutting**, page 51, to cut fabric. All measurements include ¹/₄" seam allowances.*

From assorted print fabrics:
- Cut 200 **squares** 4" x 4".

From white solid fabric:
- Cut 17 strips 6⁵/₈" wide. From these strips, cut 100 **squares** 6⁵/₈" x 6⁵/₈".

From yellow print fabric:
- Cut 7 **strips** 1¹/₈" wide.
- Cut 1 strip 3" wide. From this strip, cut 4 **squares** 3" x 3".
- Cut 8 **binding strips** 2¹/₄" wide.

ASSEMBLING THE BLOCKS

*Follow **Piecing**, page 52, and **Pressing**, page 53. Match the right sides and use a ¼" seam allowance when sewing. Measurements given throughout assembly include outer seam allowances.*

1. Draw a diagonal line (corner to corner) on wrong side of each 4" print **square**. Draw another diagonal line ¹/₂" away from first drawn line *(Fig. 1)*.

Fig. 1

2. With right sides together, place a marked **square** on two opposite corners of a $6^{5}/_{8}$" white **square**. Stitch along each drawn line *(Fig. 2)*.

Fig. 2

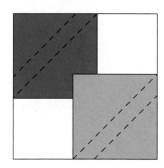

3. Cut through the center of the two stitching lines *(Fig. 3)*. Press open to make 1 **Block** and 2 **Triangle-Squares**. Make 100 **Block** and 200 **Triangle-Squares**. Blocks should measure $6^{5}/_{8}$" x $6^{5}/_{8}$". Trim Triangle-Squares to 3" x 3". (You will only use 100 of these Triangle-Squares. Save the extras to use on another project.) Set Triangle-Squares aside.

Fig. 3

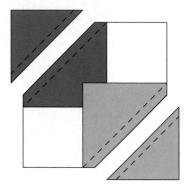

Block (make 100)

Triangle-Squares (make 200)

4. Sew 10 **Blocks** together to make a **Row**. Make 10 **Rows**. Row should measure 61³/₄" x 6⁵/₈".

Row (make 10)

5. *Refer to **Quilt Top Diagram**, page 41, to assemble the Quilt Top Center and to add the Borders.* Sew Rows together to make **Quilt Top Center**. Quilt Top Center should measure 61³/₄" x 61³/₄".

ADDING THE BORDERS
Inner Borders

1. Using diagonal seams *(Fig. 4)*, sew 1¹/₈" wide yellow print **strips** together end to end to make 1 continuous **inner border strip**.

Fig. 4

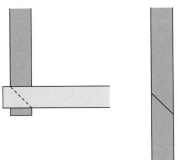

2. To determine length of **inner side borders**, measure *length* across center of quilt top center. From continuous inner border strip, cut 2 inner side borders the determined length. Matching centers and corners, sew inner side borders to quilt top center.

3. To determine length of **inner top/bottom borders**, measure *width* across center of quilt top center (including added borders). From continuous inner border strips, cut 2 inner top/bottom borders the determined length. Matching centers and corners, sew inner top/bottom borders to quilt top center.

Outer Borders

1. Sew 25 **Triangle-Squares** together to make **outer border**. Make 4 outer borders.

2. Matching centers and corners, sew 1 outer side border to each side of quilt top center.

3. Sew a 3" yellow print **square** to each end of remaining outer borders.

4. Matching centers and corners, sew outer top/bottom borders to Quilt Top Center.

COMPLETING THE QUILT

1. Follow **Quilting**, page 55, to mark, layer, and quilt as desired. The model is machine quilted with a meandering pattern.

2. If desired, follow **Adding A Hanging Sleeve**, page 59, to add a hanging sleeve.

3. Use **binding strips** and follow **Piecing Binding Strips**, page 60, and **Attaching Binding with Mitered Corners**, page 61, to make and attach **straight-grain binding**.

Outer Border (make 4)

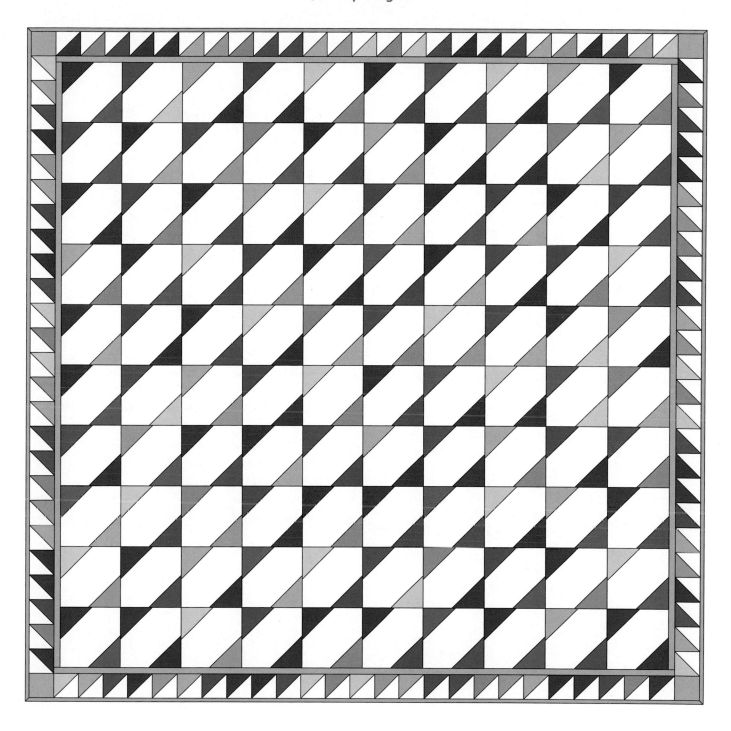

Chinese Coins

Finished Quilt Size: 68" x 81½" (173 cm x 207 cm)

CUTTING THE PIECES

*Follow **Rotary Cutting**, page 51, to cut fabric. Cut all strips across the selvage-to-selvage width of the fabric unless otherwise indicated. All measurements include ¼" seam allowances.*

From black solid:
- Cut 2 *lengthwise* **side outer borders** 8" x 81".
- Cut 2 *lengthwise* **top/bottom outer borders** 8" x 52½".
- Cut 5 *lengthwise* **sashing strips** 6" x 61½".

From assorted solid fabrics:
- Cut 1 or more **strips** from each fabric in widths varying from 1½"w to 2¼"w.

ASSEMBLING THE QUILT TOP

*Follow **Piecing**, page 52, and **Pressing**, page 53. Match the right sides and use a ¼" seam allowance when sewing. Assemble strips and units in random fabric combinations.*

1. Assemble **strips** as shown to make a **Strip Set** 21½" long. Make 3 Strip Sets. Cut across Strip Sets at 5½" intervals to make a total of 12 **Unit 1's**. Cut across remaining Strip Sets at 2¾" intervals to make a total of 11 **Unit 2's**.

Strip Set (make 3)

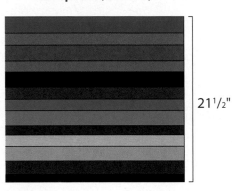

21½"

Unit 1
(make 12)

Unit 2
(make 11)

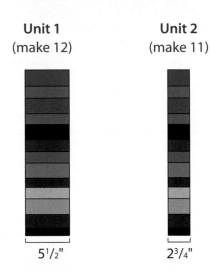

5½"   2¾"

2. Sew short edges of all Unit 1's together to make 1 **Pieced Strip**. Cut across Pieced Strip at 61½" intervals to make a total of 4 **Unit 3's**.

Unit 3 (make 4)

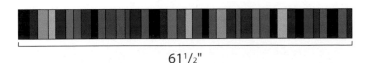

61½"

3. Refer to **Quilt Top Diagram**, page 45, to assemble **Unit 3's** and **sashing strips** to complete center section of quilt top.

4. Sew short edges of all **Unit 2's** together to make 1 **Border Strip**. Cutting across Border Strip, cut 2 **top/bottom inner borders** 48" long. Cutting across remainder of Border Strip cut 2 **side inner borders** 66" long.

Border Strip (make 1)

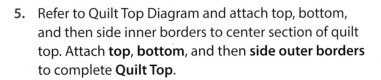

5. Refer to Quilt Top Diagram and attach top, bottom, and then side inner borders to center section of quilt top. Attach **top**, **bottom**, and then **side outer borders** to complete **Quilt Top**.

COMPLETING THE QUILT

1. Follow **Quilting**, page 55, to mark, layer, and quilt as desired. The model is hand quilted with a cable pattern on the sashing strips, straight lines on the pieced areas, and a feather pattern on the outer border.

2. If desired, follow **Adding A Hanging Sleeve**, page 59, to add a hanging sleeve.

3. Follow **Making Straight Grain Binding**, page 60, and **Attaching Binding with Overlapped Corners**, page 63, to make and attach 2½"w **straight-grain binding**.

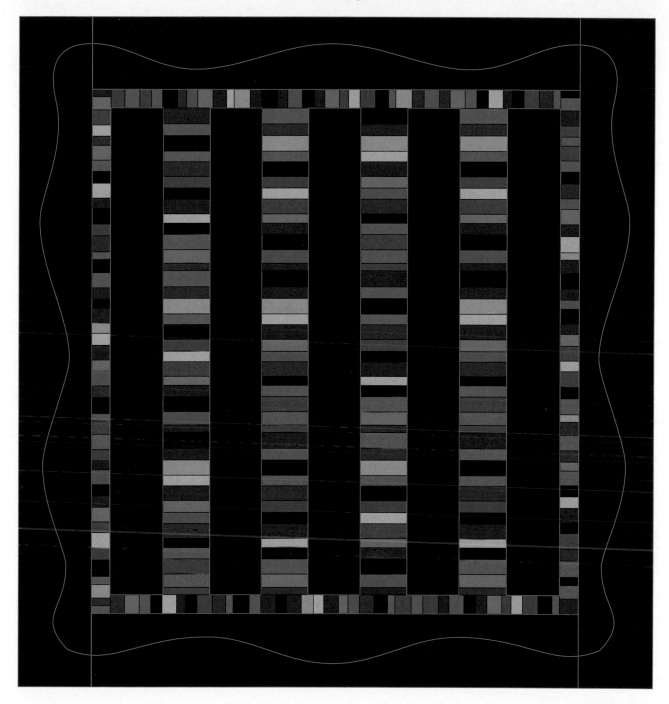

Emily's Garden in Blossom

Design by Cotton Way, Emily Olaveson.

Finished Size: 49¹/₂" x 68" (126 cm x 173 cm)

SHOPPING LIST

Yardage is based on 43"/44" (109 cm/112 cm) wide fabric with a usable width of 40" (102 cm).

- ☐ Jelly Roll* with at least 40 **strips**
- ☐ Charm Pack* with at least 36 **squares**
- ☐ 9" x 9" (23 cm x 23 cm) square of dark brown print fabric
- ☐ ⁵/₈ yd (57 cm) of fabric for binding
- ☐ 4¹/₄ yds (3.9 m) of fabric for backing
- ☐ 58" x 76" (147 cm x 193 cm) rectangle of batting
- ☐ Paper-backed fusible web

*OR
- ☐ 3³/₄ yds (3.4 m) *total* of assorted print fabrics.

CUTTING THE PIECES

*Follow **Rotary Cutting**, page 51, to cut fabric. Cut all strips from the selvage-to-selvage width of the fabric. All measurements include ¹/₄" seam allowances.*

From assorted print fabrics:
- Cut 40 **strips** 2¹/₂"w if not using Jelly Roll.
- Cut 18 **squares** 5" x 5" if not using Charm Pack.

From fabric for binding:
- Cut 7 **binding strips** 2¹/₂"w.

CUTTING THE APPLIQUÉS

*Follow **Preparing Fusible Appliqués**, page 53, and use patterns, page 49, to cut appliqués.*

From Charm Pack or assorted print fabrics:
- Cut 18 **small circles**.

From dark brown print fabric:
- Cut 1 **flower**.

*Jelly Rolls (an assortment of 2¹/₂"w strips) and Charm Packs (an assortment of 5" x 5" squares) are available at most quilt stores.

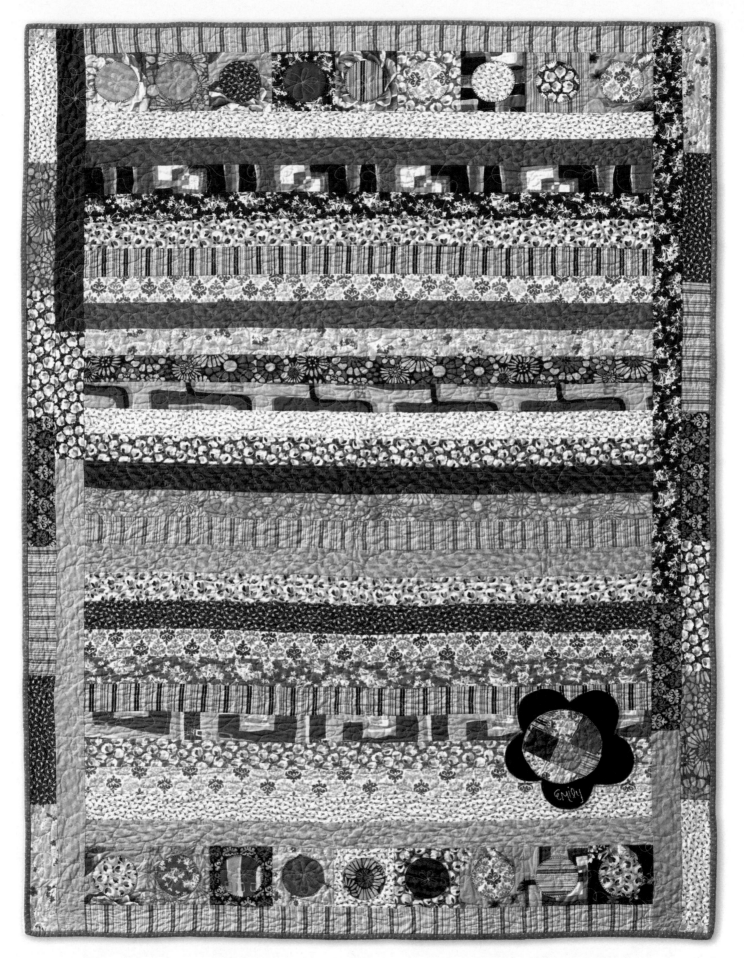

MAKING THE APPLIQUÉD BLOCKS

*Follow **Machine Blanket Stitch Appliqué**, page 53, to make Blocks.*

1. Center and fuse 1 **small circle** to each **square**. Blanket Stitch appliqué small circles to make 18 **Appliquéd Blocks**.

Appliquéd Block (make 18)

ASSEMBLING THE QUILT TOP

*Follow **Piecing**, page 52, and **Pressing**, page 53. Match the right sides and use a ¼" seam allowance when sewing. Refer to **Quilt Top Diagram** for placement.*

1. Matching long edges, sew 27 **strips** together to make **Quilt Top Center**. *Tip: Sew every other seam in the opposite direction.* Trim Quilt Top Center to 41"w.

2. Sew 9 Appliquéd Blocks together to make **top/bottom inner border**. Make 2 top/bottom inner borders.

3. Trim 2 strips to 41" long for **top/bottom outer borders**.

4. Matching centers and corners, sew top/bottom inner borders to Quilt Top Center. In the same manner, sew top/bottom outer borders to quilt top.

5. Measure length through center of quilt top (including added borders). From remaining **strips**, cut random lengths and piece together to make 4 **border strips** the determined measurement. (Set left over pieces aside.)

6. Sew 2 border strips together to make **side border**. Make 2 side borders.

7. Matching centers and corners, sew side borders to quilt top.

ADDING THE APPLIQUÉD FLOWER

1. Using leftover pieces set aside from border strips, cut 12 squares 2½" x 2½".

2. Sew 4 squares together to make **Unit 3**. Make 3 Unit 3's.

Unit 3 (make 3)

3. Staggering Units, sew 3 Unit 3's together to make **Unit 4**.

Unit 4

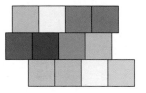

4. In the same manner as **Appliquéd Blocks**, use **large circle** pattern, page 49, to cut a circle from Unit 4. Fuse and Blanket Stitch appliqué the circle to the **flower**.

5. Fuse and Blanket Stitch appliqué the **flower** to the quilt top. If desired, use 4 strands of embroidery floss to embroider a name on the flower.

Quilt Top Diagram

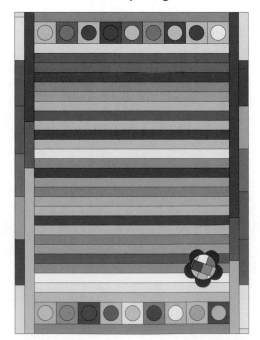

COMPLETING THE QUILT

1. Follow **Quilting**, page 55, to mark, layer, and quilt as desired. The model is machine quilted with a continuous loop and flower pattern over the entire quilt. There is a spiral quilted in the flower center.

2. If desired, follow **Adding A Hanging Sleeve**, page 59, to add a hanging sleeve.

3. Use **binding strips** and follow **Piecing Binding Strips**, page 60, and **Attaching Binding with Mitered Corners**, page 61, to make and attach **straight-grain binding**.

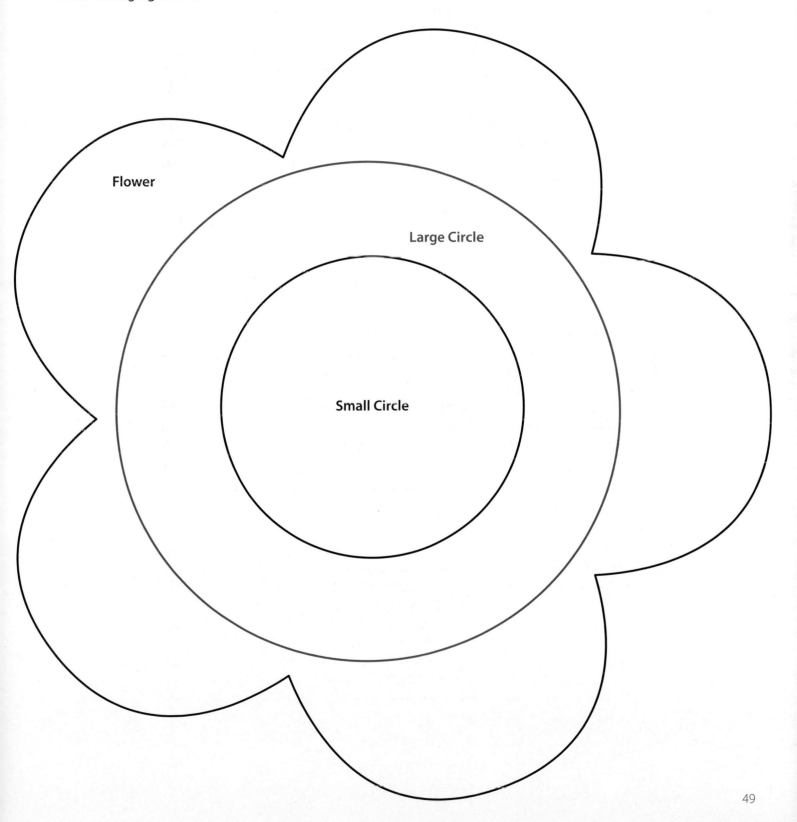

Flower

Large Circle

Small Circle

General Instructions

To make your quilting easier and more enjoyable, we encourage you to carefully read all of the general instructions, study the color photographs, and familiarize yourself with the individual project instructions before beginning a project.

FABRICS

Selecting Fabrics

Choose high-quality, medium-weight 100% cotton fabrics. All-cotton fabrics hold a crease better, fray less, and are easier to quilt than cotton/polyester blends.

Yardage requirements listed for each project are based on 43"/44" wide fabric with a "usable" width of 40" after shrinkage and trimming selvages. The actual usable width will probably vary slightly from fabric to fabric. Our recommended yardage lengths should be adequate for occasional re-squaring of the fabric when many cuts are required.

Preparing Fabrics

Pre-washing fabrics may cause the edges to ravel. As a result, your pre-cut fabric pieces may not be large enough to cut all of the pieces required for your project. Therefore, if you are using any pre-cut fabrics, we do not recommend pre-washing your yardage or pre-cut fabrics. If you are not using pre-cut fabrics, you may wish to pre-wash your fabrics.

Before cutting, prepare the fabrics with a steam iron set on cotton and starch or sizing. The starch or sizing will give the fabric a crisp finish. This will make cutting more accurate and may make piecing easier.

ROTARY CUTTING

- Place the fabric on the work surface with the fold closest to you.

- Cut all strips from the selvage-to-selvage width of the fabric unless otherwise indicated in the project instructions.

- Square the left edge of the fabric using a rotary cutter and rulers *(Figs. 1-2)*.

Fig. 1

Fig. 2

- To cut each strip required for a project, place the ruler over the cut edge of the fabric, aligning the desired marking on the ruler with the cut edge; make the cut *(Fig. 3)*.

Fig. 3

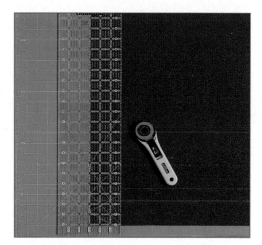

- When cutting several strips from a single piece of fabric, it is important to make sure that the cuts remain at a perfect right angle to the fold; square the fabric as needed.

PIECING

Precise cutting, followed by accurate piecing, will ensure that all pieces of the quilt top fit together well.

Hand Piecing

- Use a ruler and sharp fabric marking pencil to draw all seam lines and transfer any alignment markings onto the back of the cut pieces.

- Matching the right sides, pin two pieces together, using pins to mark the corners.

- Use Running Stitch to sew the pieces together along the drawn line, backstitching at the beginning and end of the seam.

- Do not extend the stitches into the seam allowances.

- Run five or six stitches onto the needle before pulling the needle through the fabric.

- To add stability, backstitch every ³/₄" to 1".

Machine Piecing

- Set the sewing machine stitch length for approximately 11 stitches per inch.

- Use neutral-colored general-purpose sewing thread (not quilting thread) in the needle and in the bobbin.

- An accurate ¹/₄" seam allowance is *essential*. Presser feet that are ¹/₄" wide are available for most sewing machines.

- When piecing, always place the pieces right sides together and match the raw edges; pin if necessary.

- Chain piecing saves time and will usually result in more accurate piecing.

- Trim away the points of seam allowances that extend beyond the edges of the sewn pieces.

Sewing Strip Sets

When there are several strips to assemble into a strip set, first sew the strips together into pairs, then sew the pairs together to form a strip set. To help avoid distortion, sew the seams in opposite directions *(Fig. 4)*.

Fig. 4

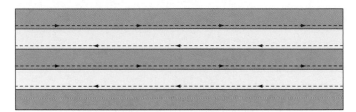

Sewing Across Seam Intersections

When sewing across the intersection of two seams, place the pieces right sides together and match the seams exactly, making sure the seam allowances are pressed in opposite directions *(Fig. 5)*.

Fig. 5

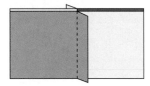

Sewing Sharp Points

To ensure sharp points when joining triangular or diagonal pieces, stitch across the center of the "X" (shown in pink) formed on the wrong side by the previous seams *(Fig. 6)*.

Fig. 6

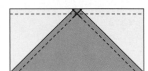

PRESSING

- Use a steam iron set on "Cotton" for all pressing.

- Press after sewing each seam.

- Seam allowances are almost always pressed to one side, usually toward the darker fabric. However, to reduce bulk it may occasionally be necessary to press the seam allowances toward the lighter fabric or even to press them open.

- To prevent a dark fabric seam allowance from showing through a light fabric, trim the darker seam allowance slightly narrower than the lighter seam allowance.

- To press long seams, such as those in long strip sets, without curving or other distortion, lay the strips across the width of the ironing board.

- When sewing blocks into rows, seam allowances may be pressed in one direction in odd numbered rows and in the opposite direction in even numbered rows. When sewing rows together, press the seam allowances in one direction.

APPLIQUÉ

Preparing Fusible Appliqués

White or light-colored fabrics may need to be lined with fusible interfacing before applying fusible web to prevent darker fabrics from showing through.

1. Place paper-backed fusible web, paper side up, over appliqué pattern. Trace pattern onto paper side of web with pencil as many times as indicated in project instructions for a single fabric.
2. Follow manufacturer's instructions to fuse traced patterns to wrong side of fabrics. Do not remove paper backing. (**Note:** Some pieces may be given as measurements, such as a 2" x 4" rectangle, instead of drawn patterns. Fuse web to wrong side of fabrics indicated for these pieces.)
3. Use scissors to cut out appliqué pieces along traced lines; use rotary cutting equipment to cut out appliqué pieces given as measurements. Remove paper backing from all pieces.

Machine Blanket Stitch Appliqué

Some sewing machines feature a Blanket Stitch similar to the one used in this book. Refer to your owner's manual for machine set-up. If your machine does not have this stitch, try a medium-width zigzag or any of the decorative stitches your machine has until you are satisfied with the look.

1. Thread sewing machine with general-purpose thread; use general-purpose thread that matches background fabric in bobbin.
2. Attach an open-toe presser foot. Select the far right needle position and needle-down setting (if your machine has this feature).
3. Pin stabilizer, such as paper or any of the widely available products, on the wrong side of the background fabric.
4. Bring the bobbin thread to the top of the fabric by lowering then raising the needle, bringing up the bobbin thread loop. Pull the loop all the way to the surface.
5. Begin by stitching 5 or 6 stitches in place (drop feed dogs or set stitch length at 0) or, if available, use your machine's lock stitch feature, to anchor the thread. Return setting to selected Blanket Stitch.
6. Most of the Blanket Stitch should be done on the appliqué with the right edges of the stitch falling at the very outside edge of the appliqué. Stitch over all exposed raw edges of appliqué pieces.
7. (*Note:* Dots on **Figs. 7-11** indicate where to leave the needle in the fabric when pivoting.) Always stopping with the needle down in the background fabric, refer to **Fig. 7** to stitch outside points, such as the tips of leaves. Stop 1 stitch short of the point. Raise the presser foot. Pivot project slightly, lower presser foot, and make angled **Stitch 1**. Take the next stitch, stop at point, and pivot so **Stitch 2** will be straight into the point. Pivot slightly to make **Stitch 3**. Continue stitching.

Fig. 7

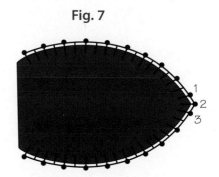

8. For outside corners *(Fig. 8)*, stitch to the corner, stopping with needle in the background fabric. Raise the presser foot. Pivot the project, lower the presser foot, and take an angled stitch. Raise the presser foot. Pivot the project, lower the presser foot, and stitch the adjacent side.

Fig. 8

9. For inside corners *(Fig. 9)*, stitch to the corner, taking the last bite at the corner and stopping with needle down in the background fabric. Raise the presser foot. Pivot the project, lower the presser foot, and take an angled stitch. Raise the presser foot. Pivot the project, lower the presser foot, and stitch the adjacent side.

Fig. 9

 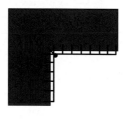

10. When stitching outside curves *(Fig. 10)*, stop with the needle in the background fabric. Raise the presser foot and pivot the project as needed. Lower the presser foot and continue stitching, pivoting as often as necessary to follow the curve.

Fig. 10

11. When stitching inside curves *(Fig. 11)*, stop with the needle in the appliqué fabric. Raise the presser foot and pivot the project as needed. Lower the presser foot and continue stitching, pivoting as often as necessary to follow the curve.

Fig. 11

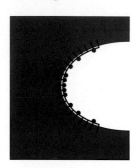

12. When stopping stitching, use a needle to pull the threads to the wrong side of the background fabric *(Fig. 12)*; knot, then trim ends, or use a lock stitch to sew 5 or 6 stitches in place.

Fig. 12

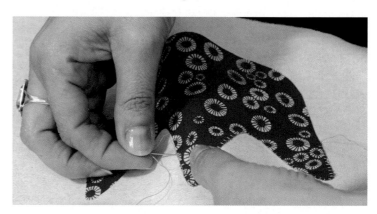

13. Carefully tear away the stabilizer, if used.

QUILTING

*Quilting holds the three layers (top, batting, and backing) of the quilt together and can be done by hand or machine. Because marking, layering, and quilting are interrelated and may be done in different orders depending on the circumstances, please read the entire **Quilting** section, pages 55-58, before beginning the project.*

Types of Quilting Designs

In the Ditch Quilting
Quilting along the seamlines or along the edges of appliquéd pieces is called "in the ditch" quilting. This type of quilting should be done on the side *opposite* the seam allowance and does not have to be marked.

Outline Quilting
Quilting a consistent distance, usually ¼", from the seam or appliqué is called "outline" quilting. Outline quilting may be marked, or ¼" masking tape may be placed along the seamlines for a quilting guide. (Do not leave the tape on the quilt longer than necessary, since it may leave an adhesive residue.)

Motif Quilting
Quilting a design, such as a feathered wreath, is called "motif" quilting. This type of quilting should be marked before basting the quilt layers together.

Echo Quilting
Quilting that follows the outline of an appliquéd or pieced design with two or more parallel lines is called "echo" quilting. This type of quilting does not need to be marked.

Channel Quilting
Quilting with straight, parallel lines is called "channel" quilting. This type of quilting may be marked or stitched using a guide.

Crosshatch Quilting
Quilting straight lines in a grid pattern is called "crosshatch" quilting. Lines may be stitched parallel to the edges of quilt or stitched diagonally. This type of quilting may be marked or stitched using a guide.

Meandering Quilting
Quilting in random curved lines and swirls is called "meandering" quilting. Quilting lines should not cross or touch each other. This type of quilting does not need to be marked.

Stipple Quilting
Meandering quilting that is very closely spaced is called "stipple" quilting. Stippling will flatten the area quilted and is often stitched in the background areas to raise the appliquéd or pieced designs. This type of quilting does not need to be marked.

Marking Quilting Lines
Quilting lines may be marked using fabric marking pencils, chalk markers, or water- or air-soluble pens.

Simple quilting designs may be marked with chalk or chalk pencil after basting. A small area may be marked, then quilted, before moving to the next area to be marked. Intricate designs should be marked before basting using a more durable marker.

Caution: Pressing may permanently set some marks. **Test** different markers **on scrap fabric** to find one that marks clearly and can be thoroughly removed.

A wide variety of pre-cut quilting stencils, as well as entire books of quilting patterns, are available. Using a stencil makes it easier to mark intricate or repetitive designs.

To make a stencil from a pattern, center template plastic over the pattern and use a permanent marker to trace the pattern onto the plastic. Use a craft knife with a single or double blade to cut channels along the traced lines *(Fig. 13)*.

Fig. 13

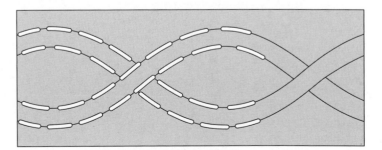

Preparing the Backing

To allow for slight shifting of the quilt top during quilting, the backing should be approximately 4" larger on all sides. Yardage requirements listed for quilt backings are calculated for 43"/44"w fabric. Using 90"w or 108"w fabric for the backing of a bed-sized quilt may eliminate piecing. To piece a backing using 43"/44"w fabric, use the following instructions.

1. Measure the length and width of the quilt top; add 8" to each measurement.
2. If the determined width is 79" or less, cut the backing fabric into two lengths slightly longer than the determined *length* measurement. Trim the selvages. Place the lengths with right sides facing and sew the long edges together, forming a tube *(Fig. 14)*. Match the seams and press along one fold *(Fig. 15)*. Cut along the pressed fold to form a single piece *(Fig. 16)*.

Fig. 14	Fig. 15	Fig. 16

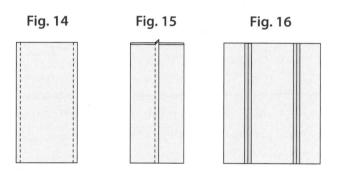

3. If the determined width is more than 79", it may require less fabric yardage if the backing is pieced horizontally. Divide the determined *length* measurement by 40" to determine how many widths will be needed. Cut the required number of widths the determined *width* measurement. Trim the selvages. Sew the long edges together to form a single piece.
4. Trim the backing to the size determined in Step 1; press the seam allowances open.

Choosing the Batting

The appropriate batting will make quilting easier. For fine hand quilting, choose low-loft batting. All cotton or cotton/polyester blend battings work well for machine quilting because the cotton helps "grip" the quilt layers. If the quilt is to be tied, a high-loft batting, sometimes called extra-loft or fat batting, may be used to make the quilt "fluffy."

Types of batting include cotton, polyester, wool, cotton/polyester blend, cotton/wool blend, and silk.

When selecting batting, refer to the package labels for characteristics and care instructions. Cut the batting the same size as the prepared backing.

Assembling the Quilt

1. Examine the wrong side of the quilt top closely; trim any seam allowances and clip any threads that may show through the front of the quilt. Press the quilt top, being careful not to "set" any marked quilting lines.
2. Place the backing *wrong* side up on a flat surface. Use masking tape to tape the edges of the backing to the surface. Place the batting on top of the backing fabric. Smooth the batting gently, being careful not to stretch or tear. Center the quilt top *right* side up on the batting.
3. If hand quilting, begin in the center and work toward the outer edges to hand baste all the layers together. Use long stitches and place basting lines approximately 4" apart *(Fig. 17)*. Smooth fullness or wrinkles toward the outer edges.

Fig. 17

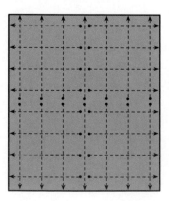

4. If machine quilting, use 1" rustproof safety pins to "pin-baste" all the layers together, spacing the pins approximately 4" apart. Begin at the center and work toward the outer edges to secure all the layers. If possible, place pins away from the areas that will be quilted, although the pins may be removed as needed when quilting.

Hand Quilting

The quilting stitch is a basic running stitch that forms a broken line on the quilt top and backing. Stitches on the quilt top and backing should be straight and equal in length.

1. Secure the center of the quilt in a hoop or frame. Check the quilt top and backing to make sure they are smooth. To help prevent puckers, always begin quilting in the center of quilt and work toward the outside edges.

2. Thread a needle with 18"-20" length of quilting thread; knot one end. Using a thimble, insert the needle into quilt top and batting approximately 1/2" from the quilting line. Bring the needle up on a quilting line *(Fig. 18)*; when the knot catches on the quilt top, give the thread a quick, short pull to "pop" the knot through the fabric into the batting *(Fig. 19)*.

3. Holding the needle with your sewing hand and placing the other hand underneath the quilt, use a thimble to push the tip of needle down through all the layers. As soon as the needle touches the finger underneath, use that finger to push the needle tip only back up through the layers to the top of the quilt. (The amount of needle showing above the fabric determines the length of the quilting stitch.) Referring to **Fig. 20**, rock the needle up and down, taking three to six stitches before bringing the needle and thread completely through the layers. Check the quilt back to make sure the stitches are going through all the layers. If necessary, make one stitch at a time when quilting through seam allowances or along curves and corners.

Fig. 20

Fig. 18

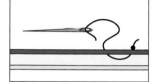

Fig. 19

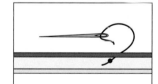

4. At the end of the thread, knot the thread close to the fabric and "pop" the knot into the batting; clip the thread close to the fabric.

5. Move the hoop as often as necessary. Thread may be left dangling and picked up again after returning to that part of the quilt.

Machine Quilting Methods

Use general-purpose thread in the bobbin. Do not use quilting thread. Thread the needle of the machine with general-purpose thread or transparent monofilament thread to make the quilting blend with the quilt top fabrics. Use decorative thread, such as a metallic or contrasting-color general-purpose thread, to make the quilting lines stand out more.

Straight-Line Quilting

The term "straight-line" is somewhat deceptive, since curves (especially gentle ones) as well as straight lines can be stitched with this technique.

1. Set the stitch length for six to ten stitches per inch and attach the walking foot to the sewing machine.

2. Determine which section of the quilt will have the longest continuous quilting line, oftentimes the area from the center top to the center bottom. Roll up and secure each edge of the quilt to help reduce the bulk, keeping the fabrics smooth. Smaller projects may not need to be rolled.

3. Begin stitching on the longest quilting line, using very short stitches for the first $1/4$" to "lock" quilting. Stitch across the project, using one hand on each side of the walking foot to slightly spread the fabric and to guide the fabric through the machine. Lock the stitches at end of the quilting line.

4. Continue machine quilting, stitching longer quilting lines first to stabilize quilt before moving on to other areas.

Free-Motion Quilting

Free-motion quilting may be free form or may follow a marked pattern.

1. Attach the darning foot to the sewing machine and lower or cover the feed dogs.

2. Position the quilt under the darning foot; lower the foot. Holding the top thread, take a stitch and pull the bobbin thread to top of quilt. To "lock" the beginning of the quilting line, hold the top and bobbin threads while making three to five stitches in place.

3. Use one hand on each side of the darning foot to slightly spread the fabric and to move the fabric through the machine. Even stitch length is achieved by using smooth, flowing hand motion and steady machine speed. Slow machine speed and fast hand movement will create long stitches. Fast machine speed and slow hand movement will create short stitches. Move quilt sideways, back and forth, in a circular motion, or in a random motion to create the desired designs; do not rotate the quilt. Lock stitches at the end of each quilting line.

ADDING A HANGING SLEEVE

Attaching a hanging sleeve to the back of a wall hanging or quilt before the binding is added allows the project to be displayed on a wall.

1. Measure the width of the quilt top edge and subtract 1". Cut a piece of fabric 7"w by the determined measurement.
2. Press the short edges of the fabric piece $1/4$" to the wrong side; press the edges $1/4$" to the wrong side again and machine stitch in place.
3. Matching the wrong sides, fold the piece in half lengthwise to form a tube.
4. Follow the project instructions to sew the binding to the quilt top and to trim the backing and batting. Before Blindstitching the binding to the backing, match the raw edges and stitch the hanging sleeve to the center top edge on the quilt back.
5. Finish binding the quilt, treating the hanging sleeve as part of the backing.
6. Blindstitch the hanging sleeve bottom to the backing, taking care not to stitch through to the quilt front.
7. Insert a dowel or slat into the hanging sleeve.

BINDING

Binding encloses the raw edges of a quilt. Because of its stretchiness, bias binding works well for binding projects with curves or rounded corners and tends to lie smooth and flat in any given circumstance. Binding may also be cut from the straight lengthwise or crosswise fabric grain.

Making Continuous Bias Strip Binding

Bias strips for binding can simply be cut and pieced to the desired length. However, when a long length of binding is needed, the "continuous" method is quick and accurate.

1. Cut a square from the binding fabric the size indicated in the project instructions. Cut the square in half diagonally to make two triangles.
2. With the right sides together and using a $1/4$" seam allowance, sew the triangles together *(Fig. 21)*; press the seam allowances open.

Fig. 21

3. On the wrong side of fabric, draw lines the width of the binding as specified in the project instructions, usually $2^{1}/_{2}$" *(Fig. 22)*. Cut off any remaining fabric less than this width.

Fig. 22

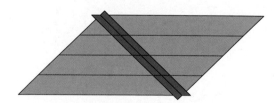

4. With the right sides inside, bring the short edges together to form a tube; match the raw edges so that the first drawn line of the top section meets the second drawn line of the bottom section *(Fig. 23)*.

Fig. 23

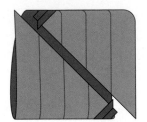

5. Carefully pin the edges together by inserting pins through the drawn lines at the point where the drawn lines intersect, making sure the pins go through the intersections on both sides. Using a ¹/₄" seam allowance, sew the edges together; press the seam allowances open.
6. To cut a continuous strip, begin cutting along the first drawn line *(Fig. 24)*. Continue cutting along the drawn line around the tube.

Fig. 24

7. Trim the ends of the bias strip square.
8. Matching the wrong sides and raw edges, carefully press the bias strip in half lengthwise to complete the binding.

Making Straight-Grain Binding

1. To determine the length of strip needed if attaching binding with mitered corners, measure the edges of the quilt and add 12".
2. To determine the lengths of the strips needed if attaching binding with overlapped corners, measure each edge of the quilt; add 3" to each measurement.
3. Cut lengthwise or crosswise strips of binding fabric the determined length and width called for in the project instructions. Strips may be pieced (see below) to achieve the necessary length.
4. Matching the wrong sides and raw edges, press the strip(s) in half lengthwise to complete the binding.

Piecing Binding Strips

1. To piece binding strips, use the diagonal seams method *(Fig. 25)*.

Fig. 25

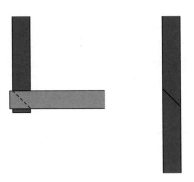

2. Matching the wrong sides and raw edges, press the strip(s) in half lengthwise to complete the binding.

Attaching Binding with Mitered Corners

1. Beginning with one end near the center on the bottom edge of the quilt, lay the binding around the quilt to make sure that the seams in the binding will not end up at a corner. Adjust placement if necessary. Matching the raw edges of the binding to the raw edge of the quilt top, pin the binding to the right side of the quilt along one edge.

2. When you reach the first corner, mark $1/4$" from the corner of the quilt top *(Fig. 26)*.

Fig. 26

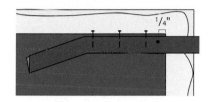

3. Beginning approximately 10" from the end of the binding and using a $1/4$" seam allowance, sew the binding to the quilt, backstitching at the beginning of stitching and at the mark *(Fig. 27)*. Lift the needle out of the fabric and clip the thread.

Fig. 27

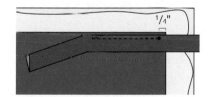

4. Fold the binding as shown in **Figs. 28-29** and pin the binding to the adjacent side, matching the raw edges. When you've reached the next corner, mark $1/4$" from the edge of the quilt top.

Fig. 28   **Fig. 29**

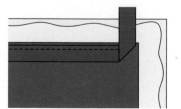

5. Backstitching at the edge of quilt top, sew the pinned binding to the quilt *(Fig. 30)*; backstitch at the next mark. Lift the needle out of the fabric and clip the thread.

Fig. 30

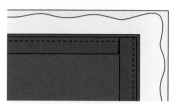

6. Continue sewing the binding to the quilt, stopping approximately 10" from the starting point *(Fig. 31)*.

Fig. 31

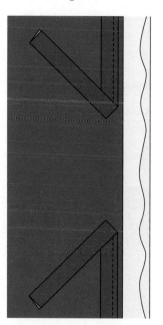

7. Bring the beginning and end of the binding to the center of the opening and fold each end back, leaving a $1/4$" space between the folds *(Fig. 32)*. Finger press the folds.

Fig. 32

8. Unfold the ends of the binding and draw a line across the wrong side in the finger-pressed crease. Draw a line through the lengthwise pressed fold of binding at the same spot to create a cross mark. With the edge of the ruler at the cross mark, line up the 45° angle marking on the ruler with one long side of the binding. Draw a diagonal line from edge to edge. Repeat on the remaining end, making sure that the two diagonal lines are angled the same way *(Fig. 33)*.

Fig. 33

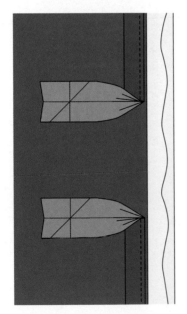

9. Matching the right sides and diagonal lines, pin the binding ends together at right angles *(Fig. 34)*.

Fig. 34

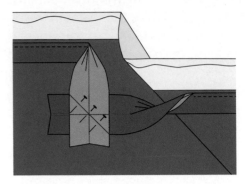

10. Machine stitch along the diagonal line *(Fig. 35)*, removing the pins as you stitch.

Fig. 35

11. Lay the binding against the quilt to double check that it is correct length.
12. Trim the binding ends, leaving a $1/4$" seam allowance; press the seam allowances open. Stitch the binding to the quilt.
13. If using $2^1/2$"w binding (finished size $1/2$"), trim the backing and batting a scant $1/4$" larger than the quilt top so that the batting and backing will fill the binding when it is folded over to the quilt backing. If using narrower binding, trim the backing and batting even with the quilt top edges.

14. On one edge of the quilt, fold the binding over to the quilt backing and pin the pressed edge in place, covering the stitching line *(Fig. 36)*. On the adjacent side, fold the binding over, forming a mitered corner *(Fig. 37)*. Repeat to pin the remainder of the binding in place.

Fig. 36   **Fig. 37**

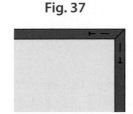

15. Blindstitch the binding to the backing, taking care not to stitch through to the quilt front.

Attaching Binding with Overlapped Corners

1. Matching the raw edges and using a $1/4$" seam allowance, sew a length of binding to the top and bottom edges on the right side of the quilt.
2. If using $2^1/2$"w binding (finished size $1/2$"), trim the backing and batting from the top and bottom edges a scant $1/4$" larger than the quilt top so that batting and backing will fill the binding when it is folded over to the quilt backing. If using narrower binding, trim backing and batting even with the quilt top edges.
3. Trim the ends of the top and bottom binding even with the quilt top edges. Fold the binding over to the quilt backing and pin the pressed edges in place, covering the stitching line *(Fig. 38)*; blindstitch the binding to the backing.

Fig. 38

4. Leaving approximately $1^1/2$" of binding at each end, stitch a length of binding to each side edge of the quilt. Trim the backing and batting as in Step 2.
5. Trim each end of the binding $1/2$" longer than the bound edge. Fold each end of the binding over to the quilt backing *(Fig. 39)*; pin in place. Fold the binding over to the quilt backing and blindstitch in place, taking care not to stitch through to the quilt front.

Fig. 39

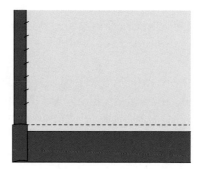

SIGNING AND DATING YOUR QUILT

A completed quilt is a work of art and should be signed and dated. There are many different ways to do this and numerous books on the subject. The label should reflect the style of the quilt, the occasion or person for which it was made, and the quilter's own particular talents. Following are suggestions for recording the history of the quilt or adding a sentiment for future generations.

- Embroider the quilter's name, date, and any additional information on the quilt top or backing. Matching floss, such as cream floss on a white border, will leave a subtle record. Bright or contrasting floss will make the information stand out.

- Make a label from muslin and use a permanent marker to write the information. Use different colored permanent markers to make the label more decorative. Stitch the label to the quilt back.

- Use photo-transfer paper to add an image to a white or cream fabric label. Stitch the label to the quilt back.

- Piece an extra block from the quilt top pattern to use as a label. Add the information with a permanent fabric pen. Appliqué the block to the quilt back.

- Write a message on an appliquéd design from the quilt top. Attach the appliqué to the quilt back.

Metric Conversion Chart

Inches x 2.54 = centimeters (cm)	Yards x .9144 = meters (m)
Inches x 25.4 = millimeters (mm)	Yards x 91.44 = centimeters (cm)
Inches x .0254 = meters (m)	Centimeters x .3937 = inches (")
	Meters x 1.0936 = yards (yd)

Standard Equivalents

1/8"	3.2 mm	0.32 cm	1/8 yard	11.43 cm	0.11 m
1/4"	6.35 mm	0.635 cm	1/4 yard	22.86 cm	0.23 m
3/8"	9.5 mm	0.95 cm	3/8 yard	34.29 cm	0.34 m
1/2"	12.7 mm	1.27 cm	1/2 yard	45.72 cm	0.46 m
5/8"	15.9 mm	1.59 cm	5/8 yard	57.15 cm	0.57 m
3/4"	19.1 mm	1.91 cm	3/4 yard	68.58 cm	0.69 m
7/8"	22.2 mm	2.22 cm	7/8 yard	80 cm	0.8 m
1"	25.4 mm	2.54 cm	1 yard	91.44 cm	0.91 m